A DAY IN THE LIFE OF A COMMUNITY SERVICE VEHICLE

A DAY IN THE LIFE OF A POLICE CAR

by Nicole A. Mansfield

PEBBLE
a capstone imprint

Published by Pebble, an imprint of Capstone
1710 Roe Crest Drive, North Mankato, Minnesota 56003
capstonepub.com

Library of Congress Cataloging-in-Publication Data is available on the Library of Congress website.
ISBN: 9780756587062 (hardcover)
ISBN: 9780756587017 (paperback)
ISBN: 9780756587024 (ebook PDF)

Summary: A police car's siren blasts. Its lights flash. Police officers depend on their cars to do their important work. Where does a police car go throughout the day? What equipment does a police car have, and how does it work? Go behind the scenes to discover how police officers use their cars from sunrise to sunset.

Editorial Credits
Editor: Carrie Sheely; Designer: Elyse White; Media Researcher: Jo Miller; Production Specialist: Tori Abraham

Image Credits
Alamy: H. Mark Weidman Photography, 14, Mark Summerfield , 9, Michael Matthews - Police Images, 8; AP Images: News Herald, Duncan Scott, 18; Capstone, 11; Getty Images: gorodenkoff, 19, kali9, 10, 15, kandypix, 17; Shutterstock: Brad Sauter, cover (front and back), Alexandr Makarov, 20 (glue), Anton Starikov, 20 (paper), MichaelJayBerlin, 20 (pen), Photo Spirit, 4, Stockjob, 7, Tohuwabohu 1976, 5, Yevhen Prozhyrko, 12, Yingna Cai, 6

Printed and bound in China. 6097

TABLE OF CONTENTS

Words in **bold** are in the glossary.

READY TO HELP

Wee-oww! Wee-oww! A car zooms by. Its red and blue lights flash. The police car is on its way to an **emergency**.

Sport utility vehicle

Police cars help in **communities**. Police officers use them as they work. They use different kinds of vehicles. Some are sport utility vehicles (SUVs).

MORNING AT THE STATION

Police cars start their morning before many people are awake. Most police cars are parked at the police station overnight.

Checking a tire's air pressure

Police officers arrive. It's time to check the cars. Do the tires have enough **tread** to grip the road? Do they have the right air **pressure** level? Do the lights work? Yes!

ON PATROL

The streets will be busy soon. The police car parks near a school. The car reminds drivers to follow speed limit and other **traffic** laws.

Next, the police car heads to its **patrol zone**. The officer sees a car that has broken down. The police car has a push bar on its front. It pushes the other car to the side of the road. Now it is not blocking traffic.

The car gets to its patrol zone. The officer uses a handheld radar. It shows the officer if cars are speeding. Officers may give **tickets** to drivers who don't follow laws.

Officers use equipment in their cars too. They might use laptops. These help officers find information during traffic stops.

AN AFTERNOON EMERGENCY!

In the afternoon, the **dispatcher's** voice comes through the car's radio. A bank robbery has been reported. The officer tells the dispatcher she is responding. The police car's lights and sirens turn on. *Zoom!* The car is on its way!

Other cars pull over as the police car speeds down the road. This gives the police car a clear path. It does not need to slow down.

The police car stops in front of the bank. Officers get out of their cars. They rush into the building.

The police officers arrest the robbery **suspects**. They are put in the police car's back seat.

A police car has a divider called a partition. Partitions help keep officers safe. People in the back seat cannot hurt officers in the front seat.

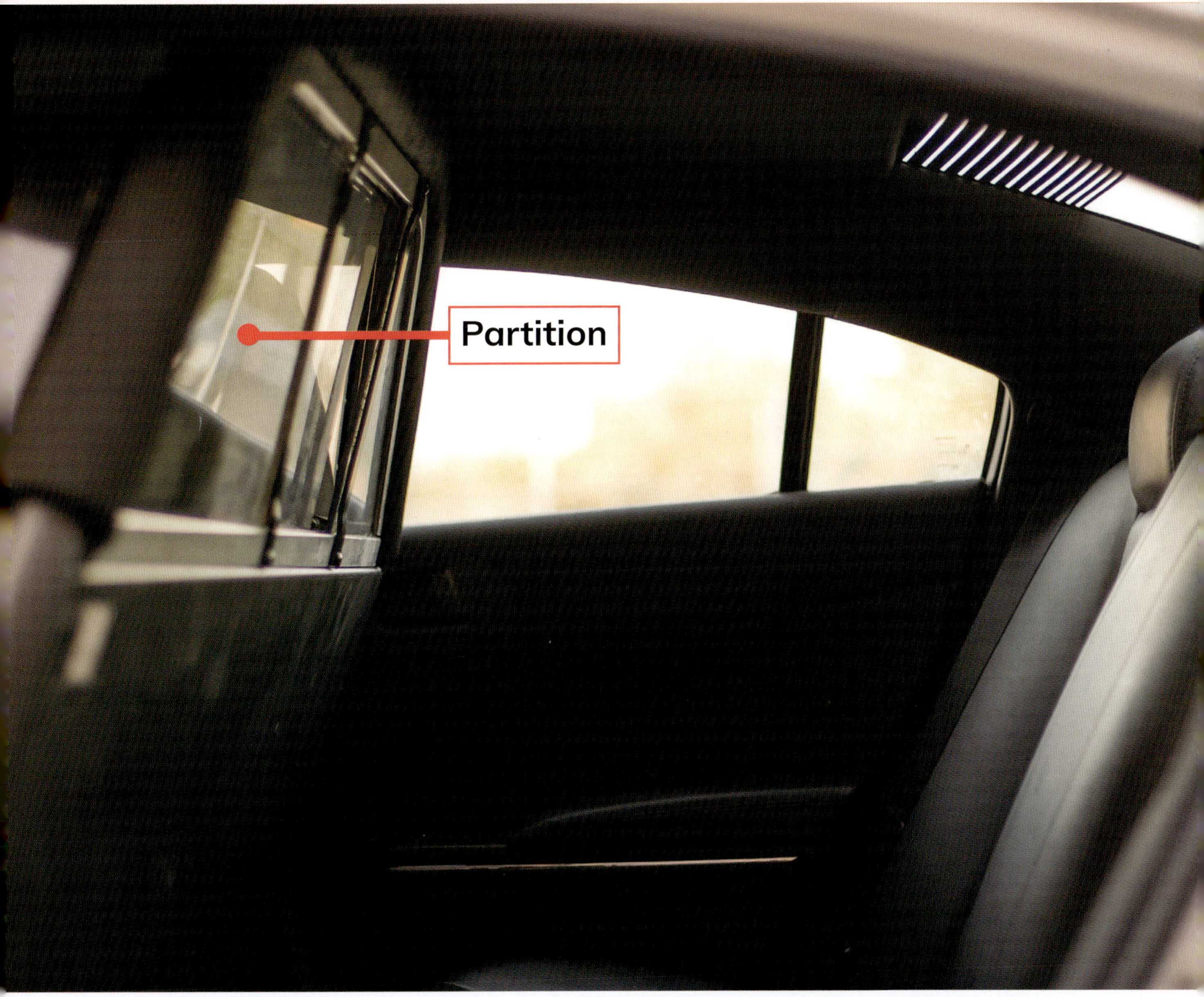
Partition

BACK TO THE STATION

The sun is going down. The police car heads back to the station. The officer fills up the car's gas tank.

Soon, the night-**shift** police officers will arrive. Police cars respond to emergencies day and night. They help keep us safe.

TORN-PAPER POLICE CAR

You've learned a lot about what police cars do in a day. Now you can make your own police car out of construction paper.

What You Need:

- black, blue, red, and white construction paper (1 sheet of each)
- black marker
- glue stick

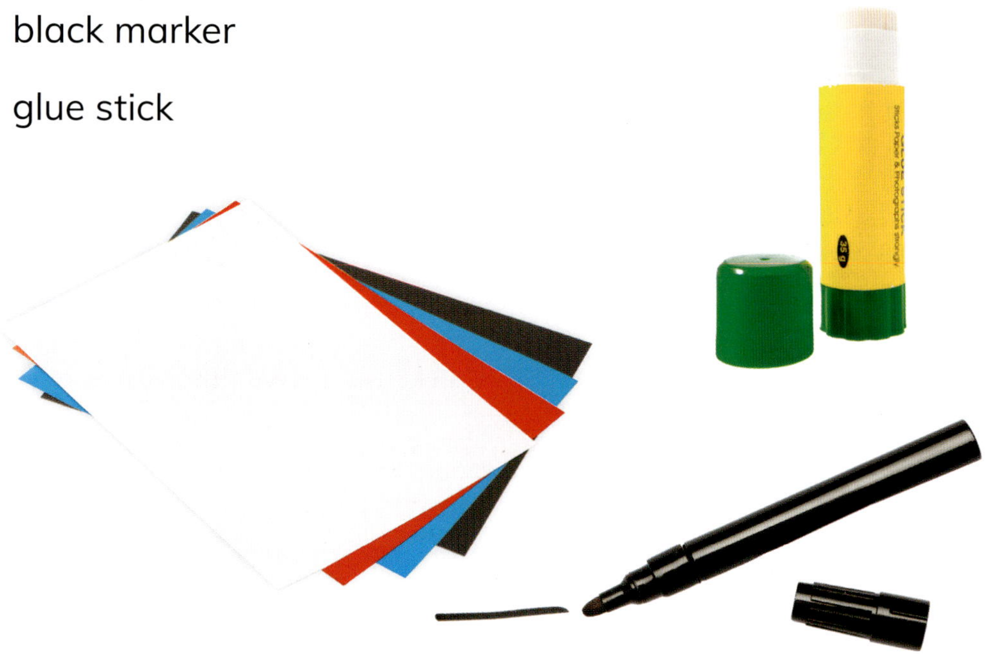

What You Do:

1. Tear a large rectangle out of the blue paper. This is the body of your police car.
2. Tear a smaller rectangle out of the white paper. This will be the car's top.
3. Glue the white rectangle on top of the blue rectangle.
4. Tear two circles out of the black paper. These will be the tires.
5. Glue the two black tires to the bottom of the car.
6. Tear two small squares out of the red paper and two small squares out of the blue paper. Glue them on top of the white rectangle. These are the car's lights.
7. Use the black marker to write "Police" on the blue construction paper.
8. Draw two rectangles on the white paper to make windows.
9. Share your artwork with your family and friends to show what you've learned.

GLOSSARY

community (kuh-MYOO-nuh-tee)—a group of people who live in the same area

dispatcher (dis-PACH-uhr)—a person who answers emergency calls and sends rescue workers

emergency (i-MUHR-juhn-see)—a sudden and dangerous situation that must be handled quickly

patrol zone (puh-TROHL ZOHN)—a certain area in which a police officer works

pressure (PRESH-ur)—the force produced by pressing on something

shift (SHIFT)—a set time period to work

suspect (SUHSS-pekt)—a person thought to be responsible for a crime

ticket (TIK-it)—a written order to pay money or go to court for breaking a traffic law

tread (TRED)—a ridge on a car's tire that helps the tire grip the road

READ MORE

McDonald, Amy. *Police Cars*. Minneapolis: Bellwether Media, Inc., 2022.

Schuh, Mari C. *All about Police Officers*. Minneapolis: Lerner Publications, 2021.

Sipperley, Keli. *Police Cars*. North Mankato, MN: Capstone, 2022.

INTERNET SITES

Kiddle: Police Car Facts for Kids
kids.kiddle.co/Police_car

PBS: Meet the Helpers: Police Officer: In-Depth
pbs.org/video/meet-the-helpers-police-officer-in-depth-pxd7ms

Tallahassee Police Department: Just for Kids!
talgov.com/publicsafety/tpd-jfk

INDEX

ABOUT THE AUTHOR

Nicole A. Mansfield is a mother of three, a wife, and educator. She enjoys singing and leading church worship music every chance that she gets! She is passionate about eating well and exercising. Nicole lives in the great state of Texas with her military family.